AM I
MAKING
MYSELF
CLEAR?

AM I
MAKING
MYSELF
CLEAR?

SECRETS OF THE WORLD'S
GREATEST COMMUNICATORS

TERRY FELBER

THOMAS NELSON PUBLISHERS®
Nashville

A Division of Thomas Nelson, Inc.
www.ThomasNelson.com

Published in Nashville, Tennessee, by Thomas Nelson, Inc.

Scripture quotations noted NRSV are from the NEW REVISED
STANDARD VERSION of the Bible © 1989 by the Division of
Christian Education of the National Council of the Churches of Christ
in the U.S.A. All rights reserved.

Scripture quotations marked NKJV are taken from the New King James
Version®. Copyright © 1982 by Thomas Nelson, Inc. Used by permission.
All rights reserved.

Library of Congress Cataloging-in-Publication Data

Felber, Terry.
  Am I making myself clear? : secrets of the world's greatest
communicators ; Terry Felber.
      p. cm.
    ISBN 0-7852-6434-5 (pb)
          0-7852-6422-1 (hc)
    1. Communication in management. 2. Communication in organizations.
  3. Business communication. 4. Interpersonal communication. I. Title.
  HD30.3.F45 2002
  153.6—dc21   2002007531

Printed in the United States of America

02 03 04 05 06 PHX 6 5 4 3 2

This book is dedicated to my best friend, my wife Linda,
who has taught me through her love and encouragement
how to serve people through thoughtful words.

ACKNOWLEDGMENTS

I want first and foremost to thank my friend John Bolin, who collaborated with me on the writing and research of this book. As we've worked together, he's been a great practitioner of the communication principles underscored here. I also want to thank my friends Bill Hawkins and Paul Tsika for their valued input. There is an old adage: There is no such thing as an original idea. Certainly the axioms for skillful communication that I've outlined in this book, I've learned from the great people that God has placed in my life. And I thank them all.

CONTENTS

CONTENTS

PREFACE

As we were both growing up, my wife Linda and I remember thinking that we wanted to live "a life of significance." We didn't want to look back at the end of our lives, regretting what could have been. We didn't want to pass through this life just existing, just putting in our time. Ron Puryear, a mentor to thousands in our business, calls this "a life of no regrets."

It became clear to us that if we were to make a difference, it would be through our relationships with others. We came to learn that much of our fulfillment in life is based on our ability to connect with people in a real way. We have come to understand that *communication skills* are the key to our success in this area.

By the grace of God we became associated with a holding company, Alticor, owned by the billionaire DeVos and Van Andel families. Over the past twenty-five years, this business vehicle has allowed Linda and me to interact with hundreds of thousands of people, whether through sports-arena presentations or through individual relationships. Our lives have been wonderfully enriched by the thousands of friendships that have ensued.

The following are excerpts from a letter I received not long ago:

I'm writing to thank you for the difference you've made in my life. I've never told you much about my past. As I was growing up, the other kids I was around made fun of my looks a lot and the fact that I was homely. I never had any friends, and kept to myself. My parents fought all the time and constantly criticized me. When I was a teenager I frequently thought about suicide. Things weren't much better as I approached thirty.

Then I met you and Linda. You talked to me like you really cared about me. You encouraged me to do more with my life, and told me you believed in me. I had never heard that before from anyone. It was like walking out of a dark building into the sunlight.

I now believe I can do great things, because of your friendship. I'm forever grateful . . .

We all have the ability to make a difference through our kind words and uplifting speech. Linda and I have had great friends and mentors in our lives, such as Theron Nelsen, Ron

Puryear, Bill Britt, and our pastor, Ted Haggard, who have equipped us with the tools whereby we are able to successfully develop impacting relationships. This book shares those communication skills with you in the hope that, through your successful relationships, you also will have *a life of no regrets*.

CHAPTER ONE

THE ART
OF COMMUNICATION

*There may be no single thing more important in our efforts
to achieve meaningful work and fulfilling relationships than
to learn to practice the art of communication.*
                    —MAX DE PREE, *Leadership Is an Art*

Abraham Lincoln is considered by many to have been the greatest American president. Winston Churchill has been regarded as the most inspiring English statesman in history. Johannes Gutenberg has been named one of the most influential men of the last millennium. And Mother Teresa is recognized the world over as an outstanding humanitarian.

What has made the lives of these individuals so different? What is it about these persons that has set them apart? Certainly it is a combination of many factors, including passion, determination, faith, circumstances, and a positive attitude.

But there is something else—a "something" rare and yet available to everyone on Earth—that turned a gangly lawyer into a world leader, changed a stuttering adolescent into a catalyst for allied peace, enabled a simple newspaperman to transform the way the world thinks, and helped a frail woman give hope to thousands.

That special "something" is the lost art of communication.

This is more than simply talking to another person. The art of communication is the dance that we have with others. It involves our words, our actions, and our intentions. It is a two-way dynamic that relies on our vigilantly watching and reading the other person in order to determine the next step. The individuals listed above all engaged in this dance, and because they did they were able to deliver their incredible gifts to the world.

A new generation of world-changers is alive today. Every one of us, including you and me, has been placed here on Earth with a special set of talents and insights that can benefit people. Don't let yourself be content to rock away your best years with drifting thoughts of what life "could have been." Grab hold of your destiny!

If we could only communicate our ideas well, our world would dramatically improve: Our jobs would become more satisfying, our bank accounts would grow, our marriages would be happier, our families would be healthier, our minds would be sharper, and our overall quality of life would be brighter.

As you read this book, I invite you to enroll in the School of Communication. As you determine not only to study these principles but also to actually apply them, I guarantee that your life will change for the better.

You're a good candidate if:

- you're a parent who would value more meaningful conversation with your teenager.

- you're a wife who would enjoy more time and attention from your spouse.

- you're a salesman who wants to close the next deal.

- you're a husband who would like more affection and zest in your marriage.

- you're a student who hopes to have your choice of jobs after graduation.

- you're an employer who would like to cut turnover.

- you want to be the person God made you to be!

This book will teach you the significance of what you say and how you say it. If you embrace and practice the skills taught in this book, your life will be transformed. The possibilities for fulfilling your potential will be limitless. Not only will you have ideas that can change the world, but also you'll have the skills to communicate them.

We've all seen the results of poor or inaccurate communication:

- poor instructions—a failed exam

- poor posture—a lost job opportunity

- poor listening—a rejected sales offer

I love this true story of professional golfer Tommy Bolt who, while playing in Los Angeles, had a caddy with the reputation for constant chatter. Before they teed off, Bolt told him,

"Don't say a word. If I ask you something, just answer 'yes' or 'no.'" During the round Bolt found the ball next to a tree. He was going to have to hit the ball under a branch and over a lake to land it onto the green. He got down on his knees and looked through the trees to size up the shot.

"What do you think?" he asked the caddy. "Five-iron?"

"No, Mr. Bolt," the caddy answered.

"What do you mean? Not a five-iron?" Bolt snorted.

The caddy rolled his eyes. "No-o-o, Mr. Bolt."

Bolt hit the ball with the five-iron, anyway, and the ball stopped about two feet from the hole. He turned to his caddy, handed him the club, and said, "What do you think about that? You can talk now."

"Mr. Bolt," the caddy replied, "that wasn't your ball."[1]

That's the way life seems to work sometimes, doesn't it? Breakdowns in communication are all too common. The primary reason families struggle is poor communication. *USA Today* recently published the eye-opening results of a study on teenagers and stress. When the teens surveyed were asked where they turn for help in times of crisis, their most popular choice was music, second was peers, and third was TV. Amazingly, moms were number thirty-one on the list and dads were number forty-eight.[2] These teenagers obviously experience little ability to connect with their parents in a meaningful way.

According to another survey, married couples have nothing to talk about after only eight years of marriage. Professor

Hans Jurgens asked 5,000 German husbands and wives how often they talked to each other. After two years of marriage, most of them managed two or three minutes of chat over breakfast, twenty minutes over the evening meal, and a few minutes more in bed. By the sixth year, this was down to ten minutes a day. A state of "almost total speechlessness" was reached after the eighth year of marriage.[3]

There is the account of a woman who went to a lawyer saying that she wanted to divorce her husband. The lawyer asked, "Do you have any grounds?" The woman said, "Yes, we have nearly three acres." He said, "No, ma'am, you don't understand. I mean do you have a grudge?" She said, "We most certainly do; it's a three-car garage." The lawyer tried again. "Maybe I'm not being specific enough. Does your husband beat you up?" The woman said, "No, I generally get up a half-hour before he does." By now the lawyer was frustrated. He said, "What I need to know, ma'am, is why you want a divorce." "Oh," she said, "that's easy. My husband just doesn't know how to communicate."

Other surveys tell us that over 80 percent of the problems people encounter at work are related to a breakdown in communication. Think of it: If we could just discover the secret to successful communication, we could avoid 80 percent of the challenges that occur in our professional lives.

The twenty-first century is alive with technology. There are more and faster means of communication today than ever before. We can send e-mails across the world in seconds. We can phone our friends from the tops of mountains. We can connect live via video to people thousands of miles away. And yet the chasm between our current situation and our future opportunities seems to grow bigger and bigger. In spite of these incredible tools of communication, we have failed to learn the *art* of communication.

My hope is that this book will build a bridge between where you are today and where you want to be. As you read this book, you will see POWER POINTS set apart in each chapter. These are specific "nuggets" of information that can be applied to your communication arsenal for immediate results. I encourage you to highlight these points and to practice them in everyday situations.

CHAPTER TWO

THE ART OF UNSPOKEN LANGUAGE

There are four ways, and only four ways, in which we have contact with the world. We are evaluated and classified by these four contacts: what we do, how we look, what we say, and how we say it.

—DALE CARNEGIE

When we study communication we usually think in terms of words and phrases. In fact, many times it's not what we say with words but what we say with our faces, our eyes, and our bodies that most impacts the listener. Knowing how to articulate and use words is a powerful weapon in negotiating your dreams. But mastering nonverbal actions in tandem with your words will render you unstoppable.

Demosthenes, the famous Roman orator, was asked, "What is the first part of oratory?"

"Action," he answered. When asked what is the second part, his answer was the same: "Action."[1] The truth is, people tend to believe actions more than words. You may have heard someone say, "His actions spoke so loudly, I couldn't hear what he said." It's true: Actions do speak louder than words.

Prudence Leith, caterer and restaurateur, tells this story in her book *Pardon Me, but You're Eating My Doily*. "My favorite catering disaster is the true story of the couple who went to the Far East on holiday. Besides their own supper, they wanted food

for their poodle that they had taken with them on their vaca-
tion. Pointing to the dog, they made international eating signs.
The waiter nodded, picked up the poodle, and set off for the
kitchen . . . only to return half an hour later with the roasted
poodle on a platter!"

This story, tragic as it is, illustrates the importance of clear
communication. As you will discover, communication is as
much *how* you say it as it is *what* you say. In the story above, the
couple consciously used nonverbal communication to get their
point across, albeit unsuccessfully. In our everyday communication with families, friends, and work relationships, we unconsciously communicate nonverbally all the time.

In fact, it's been said that we cannot *not* communicate.
This means that we are always communicating, whether we are
consciously trying to or not. The fact that we aren't talking
doesn't mean we aren't communicating. Recent studies have
shown that we communicate a mere 8 percent of what we are
trying to say through our words, and as much as 90 percent
through our actions or nonverbal activities. Think about it:

> We smile in pleasure.
>
> We wink to imply intimacy.
>
> We scowl in disgust.
>
> We stand tall in confidence.

We cower in fear.

We point in accusation.

We slump in frustration.

We nod in approval.

We shake our heads in consternation.

We raise our eyebrows in disbelief.

We frown in disapproval.

Nonverbal communication is what we "say" without words. It's the expression on our faces, our body language, our postures. It may also include the way we wear our clothes, or the silence we keep. Let's take a moment to explore how we can specifically harness the power of nonverbal communication to become a person of influence.

> *The face is the mirror of the mind, and eyes without speaking confess the secrets of the heart.*
> —JEROME, A.D. 324–420

FACIAL EXPRESSION

If the face is the mirror of the mind, then we would do well to learn to read the messages sent to us through the faces of those with whom we communicate. Have you ever had a conversation with someone, repeated back to her the words she used, only to have her say, "That may be what I said, but that's not what I meant"? Throughout history we have tried to read the minds of others. Palm readers, hypnotists, psychiatrists, and even polygraph tests have all attempted to read minds. Truly, the greatest mechanism for determining what a person is thinking, without his actually saying it, is to observe his face! Facial expression communicates more about what we are thinking than anything else does, including words. Facial expression, "the mirror of the mind," consists of our smiles, our eyes, and our overall countenances.

> **POWER POINT:**
> A smile is contagious. Be a carrier.

If you're not using your smile, you're like a man with a million dollars in the bank, and no checkbook.

—LES GIBLIN

A winning smile is more valuable than gold. Your smile can earn you millions, save your marriage, or change a nation. A smile communicates approval, love, appreciation, and innocence. And besides, it's more work to frown than to smile. It takes sixty-two muscles to frown, and only twenty-six to smile.[2]

A broad smile is one of the greatest assets you could ever ask for. It's your way of telling the world that you're grateful to be alive. A smile has a way of drawing people in, making them comfortable, and winning them over.

A constant frown has the opposite effect. Some people travel through life with a perpetual frown on their face, and yet they don't understand why they can't get ahead. The next time you observe someone who isn't progressing in life, take a look at his face. Chances are, this "unlucky" one has unsettled issues in life and has determined to make everything a big deal. He walks around with a scowl, looking as if he's swallowed a pickle.

The management of Holiday Inn understands the value of a great smile. When looking for 500 people to fill positions for a new facility, the company interviewed 5,000 candidates. The hotel managers conducting the interviews rejected every candidate who smiled less than four times during the interview. It pays to smile!

Our smile is important in more than just business settings. Most of us men remember the first time we discovered the power of a smile. We were boys in junior high school. All a girl had to do was smile at us, and we were ready for marriage. There's nothing more attractive than a great smile! All that my wife Linda has to do is smile at me, and I'm putty in her hands.

If you aren't the type of person who smiles regularly, learn to. Practice if you have to. This might sound a bit strange, but it will be well worth it. Stand in front of your mirror and practice smiling the biggest, most attractive smile that you can. Then try out that smile on your boss, your coworkers, and your family. You'll be amazed at the results.

POWER POINT:
Learn the language of the eyes

An animal will always look for a person's intentions by looking them right in the eyes.

—H. POWERS

The eyes are the windows to the soul. Have you ever noticed that you can see right into a person through his or her eyes? That's how we've been created. Our eyes are powerful tools of communication.

Eyes twinkle with excitement, redden and tear up with sadness, and glower with hostility. Victor Hugo once said, "When a woman is speaking to you, listen to what she says with her eyes." Steve Rubenstein put it this way, "Women speak two languages, one of which is verbal." This is true. And it's as true for men as it is for women. With our eyes we can engage, connect, or remove ourselves from a conversation. Any public speaker can tell you the value of "connecting" through the eyes.

While it's important to connect through eye contact, it's also important to learn how to read other persons' expressions during conversation. I remember learning this the hard way. When my wife Linda gave birth to our son David, I remember walking into the recovery room after a couple of hours to "catch her up" on some work from the office. Linda and I are business partners, so we are constantly working together to ensure that our business is running smoothly. And so, being the considerate husband that I am, I figured I'd give her a couple of hours of rest before I approached her with some work-related issues. I can still remember the look in her eyes as I walked through the doorway of her hospital room with an armful of papers. It was a look that all women must learn from their mothers. I still have the singe marks on my cheeks. As I backed myself out of the door, I was reminded of how expressive eyes can be.

POWER POINT:
Look people in the eyes.

Many of us can remember our parents telling us to "look people in the eyes." Have you ever met someone who wouldn't look you in the eyes? You know—the kind of person that shifts his eyes back and forth simply to avoid contact. This kind of behavior elicits distrust. Have you ever greeted someone whose eyes hit the floor as he or she said hello? This behavior conveys a bad self-image.

When you really want to connect with people, make a conscious effort to look them in the eyes. Now, it's all right to blink every once in a while—you don't want people to feel uncomfortable. But it's important to artfully communicate interest and respect by making eye contact with them regularly.

In a later chapter I'll discuss the importance of listening. Keep in mind that nonverbal communication is always a two-way interaction. This means that how you "listen" with your eyes is as important as how you "talk" with them. Making eye contact infers interest, value, and intimacy. Avoiding eye contact communicates apathy, discomfort, or disagreement. Be sure to say the right thing with your eyes. If you're not used to looking people in the eyes, this may be a challenge for you. But if you work at it, you'll reap the benefits of great communication!

POWER POINT:
Wear success on your face.

Our faces contain thousands of muscles. And our faces can communicate thousands of different emotions, feelings, and attitudes. Determine to wear positive expressions on your face.

Do you remember your mother ever telling you that if you made a "bad" face and you kept doing it, it would stay like that? Well, she was right! Our faces actually do maintain muscle and tissue memory, and the face that we wear most of the time begins to stay with us. Some people wear a chronic expression that says, "Life has dealt me a bad hand," while others maintain a visage that says, "I find joy in every day." The latter are the sort of people we like to be around, and the sort of people we want to be like.

BODY LANGUAGE

What we do with our bodies during conversation communicates volumes to others. Many times, not meaning to, we say something completely different with our bodies than we do with our mouths. Psychologist Albert Mehrabian has said, "Seven percent of a speaker's message comes through his words, 38 percent comes from his title or position, and 55 percent from his 'body language.'"[3] It's clear that our bodies have an amazing ability to communicate what our minds are trying to say. In fact, sometimes our bodies can communicate what our mouths are unable to say.

After being married for more than twenty-five years, my wife Linda and I have developed a vast array of nonverbal signals. I can look across the room and have an entire conversation with her without ever saying a word. I can sit next to her at a dinner gathering with friends and interact with her under the table. (I have bruises on my legs to prove it!)

POWER POINT:
Face others directly.

If you want to build trust in a relationship, make sure you use appropriate body language. When you speak to someone, face him or her directly—nose to nose, toes to toes—rather than at an angle. With the latter, you may appear to be giving that person the "cold shoulder." Keep in mind that if you are dealing with foreign cultures, the distance considered appropriate varies, depending on where you are. For example, if you are in a European country, the personal space considered polite is at least two feet, while in many Asian countries one foot or less is not uncommon.

The power of body language can be clearly assessed by the following test: Stand in front of a group and say, "Watch me and do what I ask you to do. Make a circle with your thumb and forefinger, like this. Now put this circle on your *chin*." (As you say this, put the circle on your *cheek*.) Many will put the circle on their cheeks rather than on their chins, showing that they were following your body language rather than your words.

POWER POINT:
Good posture exudes good self-esteem.

Good posture is not only important for good health, but it can be a key to getting your next job, sale, or date. Medical doctors have been telling us about the importance of good posture for decades, and now we're beginning to see the results. People who make a conscious effort to stand up straight, to walk deliberately, and to hold their heads high actually do end up with fewer medical problems in their joints, bones, and muscles. It's more than just good business; it's good health!

And let's not underestimate the power of good posture in business. The founder of the Ralston Purina company, William Danforth, used to say, "When a man sits straight, I believe he thinks straight."[4] When a person slouches, he or she communicates a lack of self-confidence. People who are tall often hunch over to compensate for their height. Be confident in who you are. Stand up tall and strong. It's amazing how much our bodies reflect how we think, and subsequently how we live. Here's a good "posture check": Stand up against a flat wall, and see how much of your body touches the wall. You're in good shape if your shoulders, your backside, and the heels of your feet are touching the wall.

Determine to do whatever it takes to develop good posture.

For the next few days, concentrate on squaring your shoulders and pulling your chin up, your head back, and your abdomen in. A few simple exercises in the morning will do wonders for your posture.

POWER POINT:
Develop a winning handshake.

One of the best things you can do to enhance your body language is to develop a winning handshake. It's important to offer a handshake that's not too soft or too strong. A weak handshake indicates a lack of confidence, and a vice-grip handshake implies arrogance or low self-esteem.

I remember teaching my son David, at age six, how to greet someone for the first time. We practiced shaking hands, looking each other in the eyes, and standing up straight and tall. The first time we attempted the greeting, David shuffled into the room with his head down and weakly reached out his hand to shake mine. It felt like I was holding a dead fish. I then explained that his handshake needed to be firm. He grabbed my hand and squeezed it with all his strength, taking me to my knees. I then suggested that his handshake be somewhere in the middle. Do what David and I did, and practice looking people in the eyes as you shake their hands.

Become aware of the nonverbal dimensions of your communication, and apply the principles covered in this chapter. Your ability to interact and connect successfully with people will be greatly enhanced. Correspondingly, this will create more rewarding relationships.

CHAPTER THREE

THE ART
OF APPEARANCE

Regardless of how you feel inside, always try to look like a winner.

—ARTHUR ASHE

The number-one reason people will buy a book is the title; the number-two reason is the cover artwork; the third motivation is the author's name; and somewhere down near the bottom of the list is the actual content of the book. We've all heard the expression, "You can't judge a book by its cover," and to a point we would probably agree. But in fact, we do judge a book by its cover. Certainly, we may discover a great piece of literature under a shabby cover, or we might be fooled into buying sub-par writing simply because of fancy artwork on the front. But in the end, most of us will make our initial buying decision based on the cover of the book.

The same is true with people. We almost always "judge" people by our first impressions. Emily Post puts it this way: "Clothes are to us what fur and feathers are to beasts and birds; they not only add to our appearance, but they are our appearance. The first impression that we make depends largely on what we wear, including our facial expression. Manners and speech are noted afterward, and character is discerned last of all."[1]

Granted, those first impressions may turn out to be inaccurate indicators. But we do make certain decisions about people based on our initial impressions. For example, if a person walks into your office wearing sloppy clothes, exhibiting uncombed hair, and in obvious need of a shower, you'll probably make some assumptions about that person. You might think that he or she doesn't have a good sense of business etiquette—or, even worse, a healthy self-esteem.

> **POWER POINT:**
> You never get a second chance
> to make a first impression.

As you begin to master the skills of communication, it is important that you learn the secrets to presenting *yourself* as well as your ideas. Your appearance in business meetings, interviews, or even on a date will communicate as much as what you say. The two main areas of appearance are grooming and dress.

GROOMING

Here are a few things to keep on your mental grooming checklist for your next appointment, date, or presentation:

- It may go without saying, but bathing is a must.

- Keep your teeth well brushed. If you have stained or yellow teeth, use a tooth whitener. If you have crooked, gapped, or unsightly teeth, consider getting dental work that might make your smile more attractive.

- Keep your fingernails trimmed and cleaned. Women's manicures should be tasteful, not gaudy.

- Keep your hair neat and in order. Greasy, matted hair can put people off. Even if the "messy look" is in fashion, be conscious of what you are communicating to those around you. If coloring or highlighting helps your appearance, then by all means it's a good investment. I often say that the less hair you have on your head and your face, the more relatable you'll be with the most people. As I'm balding, I seem to get more relatable every year!

- The purpose of makeup is to enhance your looks, not to change them. Use it sparingly and modestly. Stay away from the "painted" look.

- Colognes and perfumes are helpful. Just make sure the fragrance isn't overbearing.

- Be sure to use deodorant or antiperspirant.

- Always keep mints with you. A person who is overwhelmed with your bad breath won't hear a word you say. Many years ago, when Linda and I were in the process of building a house, people warned us that we would have many disagreements in the process of the many decisions we would be making. But in reality we had a wonderful time creating our dream. The only arguments we ever had involved whose turn it was to meet one businessperson, because she had very bad breath. "No, Linda, I'm sure it's your turn to meet with her. I met with her last time." Maybe that's why she did so much business—people would buy whatever she suggested just to get away from her!

POWER POINT:
Clothing always communicates.

DRESSING FOR SUCCESS

What are you trying to communicate by how you look? "I just got out of bed." "I'm the most successful employee here." "I don't care what you think, I can behave the way I want." Or, "I'm interested in how I relate to you." Don't fool yourself into thinking that you haven't said a lot about yourself just by walking into a room. Other people will assess your position, your purpose, and your potential for success the minute you step through the door. Be aware how you look from the top of your head to the soles of your shoes.

Many people think to themselves, "When I become successful, I'll invest more money in a sharp wardrobe." That's like sitting in front of a fireplace and thinking, "When you get me warm, I'll feed you wood." No, you must first dress for success—then you'll become successful.

As we move at warp speed through the twenty-first century, the line between formal and casual is being constantly blurred. Given the ever-moving target of corporate dress standards, how do you know what to wear and when? Here are some guidelines for dressing on the job.

Although it seems to be what clothiers want, following every fashion trend is generally not a good idea. There is something very professional about traditional, classic attire. Stay away from elaborate or overly exaggerated fashion. Simple clothing that becomes you is best. When you dress, remember that your goal is to be able to relate to as broad a spectrum of people as possible. You don't want your appearance to hinder open communication.

POWER POINT:
Overdressing is better than underdressing.

If you're a man, choose ties with simple patterns. Stay away from mermaids, cartoon characters, and bowling pins. In other words, keep those company Christmas ties neatly packed away for a cold day when you need a few laughs. Also, dress shirts should have a tight, crisp look.

As you know, appropriate dress will vary depending on the occasion or audience. If you are dressing for an average workday, smart-casual attire might be fully acceptable. But if you are dressing for a special department presentation, a suit and tie might be more appropriate. Of course, every corporate culture in America is somewhat unique in its dress standards. For example, if you are a top executive at IBM, a suit is almost always expected. But if you work at a high-tech firm in Silicon Valley, the appropriate attire might be jeans and an open-collared shirt. At the very least, overdressing is better than underdressing, as it shows that you are considering the other person and holding him or her in high esteem.

The variation in clothing styles and how they affect work performance is interestingly illustrated in the highest office of the land. President Bill Clinton was known for working in the Oval Office in a sweat suit, while his predecessor, George W. Bush, always wore a suit coat. After the first one hundred days of President Bush's administration, the word had spread that business attire was the appropriate choice for the Oval Office. Interestingly, productivity significantly increased. In studies of high-school students, it has been noted that young people who wear uniforms to school universally outperform students that do not.

Wear clothes that enhance what you have. Wear clothes that fit you and aren't outworn. Some simple maintenance of your clothes and shoes will help them last a long time. One of my friends has worn the same shoes for thirty years, keeping them regularly polished and occasionally resoled. Keep your shoes shined. They are often one of the first things a person notices at a job interview. It also pays to have your clothing specially tailored for your body. Quality clothing and shoes will pay off when you take care of them.

POWER POINT:
Keep your clothes looking their best.

Find a good dry cleaner. Looking neat and pressed makes a big difference. A sharply dry-cleaned shirt is unmistakable. The rumpled look has never been "in," and probably never will be. If a button falls off, sew it back on. Fix any tears. Ladies, never wear pantyhose with tears or runs. Good clothing misses its mark if it has holes or stains.

If you're not sure what to buy or what looks good on you, take a well-dressed friend with you on your next shopping trip. A wise shopper doesn't have to spend a fortune on a new wardrobe each season, but just a little for a few new items to add to the standard clothing he or she already owns.

A few additional fashion tips:

- Horizontal stripes will tend to make you look bigger than you are.

- Vertical stripes will tend to make you look thinner than you are.

- Black is always a thinning color.

- Solid colors are usually better than plaids for business events.

- Women: Avoid high hemlines and low necklines. Tight-fitting and revealing clothing may communicate a message you don't intend to send. Always attempt to maintain a professional appearance that communicates your intent.

> **POWER POINT:**
> Maintain your target weight, and you'll communicate with more confidence.

The only way to keep your health is to eat what you don't want, drink what you don't like, and do what you'd rather not.

—MARK TWAIN

If you find yourself putting on unnecessary pounds, develop the discipline necessary to lose unwanted weight. Obesity makes it more difficult to communicate with confidence. It also distracts people from what you're saying. Everyone can find the appropriate target weight that will make him or her comfortable, healthy, and confident. This may mean putting yourself on a healthy, balanced diet and establishing a routine of exercise. Good health is as much a part of a good appearance as anything else.

Most of us wait until it's too late to begin thinking about eating right and exercising our bodies. In fact most people, when they have a heart attack, experience denial. "This isn't happening to me. This is a bad dream. I must have misunderstood the doctor." Not many people are like Field Marshall Montgomery. After World War II, while sitting at the House of Lords, he calmly turned to the man next to him and said, "Excuse me, but I'm having a coronary thrombosis." He quietly walked out to find medical help. Most of us continue what we're doing until we collapse. Too many of us ignore the warning signs of bad health and continue with bad habits until it's too late.

If you think contact lenses or laser surgery will help build your confidence, it is well worth the investment. When you feel better about the way you look, you'll communicate with confidence, and chances are you'll get the job, account, or date you've been dreaming of. Start today—you'll be glad you did.

POWER POINT:
Accept what you can't change.

A recent survey asked the question: "If you could change one thing about yourself, what would you change?" Nearly 90 percent of those surveyed pointed to things that they could not possibly alter.[2] The truth is that many of us are born with characteristics we may not be able to change, such as the color of our skin, our height, our bone structure, or a birth defect. If you can't change a characteristic, learn to love it and to live with it.

If you think your physical limitations in life will keep you from fulfilling your greatest potential, consider this:

In 1959, a Universal Pictures executive dismissed Clint Eastwood with the following statement: "You have a chip on your tooth, your Adam's apple sticks out too far, and you talk too slow."

John Milton became blind at age forty-four. Sixteen years later he wrote the classic *Paradise Lost*.

After years of progressive hearing loss, at age forty-six German composer Ludwig van Beethoven had become completely deaf. Nevertheless, it was after the age of forty-six that he wrote his greatest music.

After having lost both legs in an airplane crash, British fighter pilot Douglas Bader rejoined the British Royal Air Force with two artificial limbs. During World War II he was captured by the Germans three times—and three times he escaped.

Franklin D. Roosevelt was paralyzed by polio at age thirty-nine. Yet he went on to become one of America's most beloved and influential leaders. He was elected President of the United States four times.

Don't hide behind a limitation in the way you look. Use it to shout to the world that you love life.

God, grant me the serenity to accept the things I cannot change, the courage to change the things I can, and the wisdom to know the difference.
—ALCOHOLICS ANONYMOUS PRAYER

CHAPTER FOUR

THE ART
OF VALUING OTHERS

*The greatest gift that we can give one another is rapt atten-
tion to one another's existence.*
—SUE ATCHLEY EHAUGH

By the time you read this chapter, you are beginning to
develop the tools you need to become a master communicator. We have discussed the importance of nonverbal communication and appearance as important elements in developing
good communication skills. It's been said that communication
is the material with which we build our relationships.

Seek first to understand, then to be understood.
—STEVEN COVEY

As we have observed, communication is the transfer of information from one person to another. We know that for communication to be effective it must, by definition, be received by
the other person. It's one thing to work hard at posture, body
language, and facial expression in order to deliver our message
clearly to another person. But if he or she doesn't believe that
we genuinely mean what we're saying, our message falls short of
its intended target. In other words, in order for our communication to be effective we have to learn to develop a *genuine
interest* in the persons we are trying to communicate with.

During the first year that Linda and I spoke in seminars to large groups of people, Linda would get very nervous and end up vomiting right before her talks. After about a year, one day I saw her on stage giggling and laughing, looking very relaxed. She hadn't even thrown up! "Linda," I asked, "What happened today? You didn't seem at all nervous."

Here's what she said: "I finally stopped worrying about myself and started thinking how I could help these other people." Not only did Linda's sincere concern for her audience make her a more effective speaker, but she also felt happier and more at ease.

In a recent study of United States presidents, conducted by Harvard Business School, the most effective presidents were found to have had five specific character traits and skills:

1. Self-awareness

2. Self-motivation

3. Self-regulation

4. Empathy for others

5. Social skills

Interestingly, all the traits on this list relate to communication, either in the way we manage our own psyches, emotions, and bodies, or in the way we manage other people's feelings and needs. This clearly demonstrates that strong leadership is closely tied to good communication skills.

Let's take a moment to focus on the fourth point: empathy for others. Empathy is a genuine understanding of someone else's situation. Empathy is not as much a skill as it is a character trait that, when used effectively and genuinely, will deliver incredible results:

- Leaders with empathy win followers.

- Parents with empathy win their children.

- Employers with empathy win their employees.

The good news about empathy is that it is a character trait that everyone can possess and use. Empathy requires little except our ability to see situations, conversations, and relationships beyond how they impact us. It is the epitome of being others-focused rather than self-focused.

There's something innate in us that looks out for our own interests before those of others. If I take a photograph of a group you are with, who is the first person you'll look for in the picture? Yourself, of course! You'll think to yourself, *Look at my hair! It's all messed up! And my eyes are half-closed. Look at that crooked smile on my face.* The most important person to you is yourself. If we can understand that all people feel this way, and fill the need they have to be recognized and appreciated, it will open up the lines of communication in a wonderful way. Here's a great example of how empathy can be used to communicate volumes.

British statesman and financier Cecil Rhodes, whose fortune was used to endow the world-famous Rhodes Scholarships, was a stickler for correct dress. A young man who was invited to dine with Rhodes arrived late by train. He had to go directly to Rhodes's home in his travel-stained clothes. Once there, he was appalled to find that the other guests were already assembled, wearing full evening dress. After what seemed like a long time, Rhodes appeared. Even though he was obsessive about proper wardrobe, he wore a shabby old blue suit. Later the young man learned that his host had been dressed in evening clothes, but had put on the old suit when he heard of his young guest's dilemma.

Mr. Rhodes understood that demonstrating empathy for the young man would communicate more than he could ever express in words. He communicated that he was concerned about the young man's welfare and dignity.[1]

In his classic leadership book, *The Seven Habits of Highly Effective People*, Steven Covey puts it this way: "Seek first to understand, then to be understood." Others call this "listening for the customer's needs." Genuine concern for others will win friends and influence the way people connect with you.

POWER POINT:
Develop a genuine interest in others.

Seeing situations from the viewpoint of others and learning to be genuinely others-focused, is not only good practice in conversation and communication, it's a good business decision. Any accomplished salesman can tell you the importance of discovering the other person's needs and finding a way to address them. Faking interest or concern won't work. But *authentic* empathy can transform you into a world-class communicator as well as a success in business. Consider the following story as a poignant reminder of the value of demonstrating empathy.

The great United States general Colin Powell recalls a meeting with former President Ronald Reagan and certain members of his Cabinet, where a new policy that had been created by General Powell and several cabinet members was being discussed. President Reagan strongly disagreed with the details of the policy, but was determined to trust the men he had selected. He was willing to allow General Powell and the others to move forward with their proposal, mostly because he trusted them and had empowered them to make decisions. The policy was adopted, but within a few weeks it met with failure.

A press meeting was called and the media assembled to question President Reagan on the failed policy. After an intense press conference, one media representative asked the President candidly, "Was this a policy formed by you, or was someone else responsible for creating this mess?"

Without hesitating, President Reagan responded, "Absolutely it was my idea. But I'll tell you something about this ole dog. I might make a mistake one time, but I'll never make the same mistake twice." With that, he protected the reputations of his Cabinet and General Powell, and rescued them from the public's wrath. General Powell remembers standing in the pressroom with tear-filled eyes, determined to serve President Reagan the rest of his life.

This is the power of making decisions for the good of others. This is the power of a great communicator. That was one of the secrets of Ronald Reagan. He had a sincere concern for the welfare of others.

Empathy is a learned skill. Most of us are naturally self-oriented rather than others-oriented. Like any skill, empathy is something that can be learned if you apply time and effort. Think for a moment about your wonderful two-year-old Johnny as he plays with your friend's two-year-old child. Suddenly you're shocked as Baby Johnny hits the other child on the head, grabs a toy from him, and says "mine!" Johnny has to be trained to share and care about others—it's not his natural tendency. We're the same way; we have to train ourselves to genuinely care for others. Here are a few steps you can take to demonstrate to others that you are genuinely interested in them, and in so doing develop your own capacity for empathy:

1. Remember the other person's name.
2. Respond to messages quickly.
3. Make what matters to that person matter to you.

POWER POINT:
Remember people's names.

It's been said that there is no sound sweeter to the ears than the sound of one's own name. We love to hear someone mention our names. It tells us we are important to that person. You've probably noticed that when you remember someone else's name, he or she tends to respond with warmth and openness. If you really want to win someone to you, remember the names of his or her spouse and children. You might say, "But I'm just not good at names." Most of us aren't naturally good at remembering names. You must *choose* to be better with names by working at it. Learn to associate certain things with people's names to help you recall them. If you've just met someone, try repeating his name back to him several times in your initial conversation. You'll be amazed at how much better you'll be at remembering his name later.

One of my business associates has developed the skill of remembering people's names. He regularly uses this acquired skill to develop his business and win people to him. In fact, I remember being in a meeting with him one time where he met a group of people, shook their hands, and then left the room. Remarkably, a year later when he met those same individuals again, he remembered every name without skipping a beat. Do you think those people felt valued by him? Not only did they feel valued, they also felt connected, simply because someone had remembered their names.

POWER POINT:
Respond to messages quickly.

The time period in which we respond to a message—whether by phone, fax, or e-mail—communicates how much we value the other person. As a general rule, it is best to answer messages within twenty-four hours. A quick response tells the other person that he or she is important to you, and that his or her concern has been understood. We've all experienced the feeling of being "left on hold" by someone. When we fail to respond in a timely manner to other peoples' messages, it clearly says that their situation is not important to us and that what we are doing is more important. Regardless of the outcome of a quick response, the practice will earn you a reputation of accountability, consideration, and interest—a winning combination. It is also a good practice to send a note of appreciation when someone has given you a gift, rendered you a special service, or participated in a requested meeting.

One of the ways Linda and I have kept the romance alive in our marriage is to regularly write each other mushy, gushy "love-notes." Mine are usually homemade, where I draw on the card stick figures of Terry and Linda talking to each other. Linda, on the other hand, will spend hours down at the local card store picking out just the right message. In her mind, if her card doesn't elicit a tear in my eye, she hasn't done a good job as a wife. I learned long ago to always keep her card on my desk in plain view for at least two days. (In our early marriage, I threw out the cards after I read them. Big mistake!) Then, when it's time for me to discard her love-note, I walk two houses down to our neighbor's trash bin!

> **POWER POINT:**
> Make what matters to that person
> matter to you.

As you work to develop relationships at home and work, one key in establishing good communication is to make what matters to others matter to you. Birthdays, anniversaries, and other personal interests are valuable relational treasures in developing good communication skills. Take time to discover what a person's feelings are on a particular subject. At the heart of empathy lies a genuine interest in the other people.

This principle is especially helpful in dealing with family relationships. If you, as a parent, make what matters to your teenager matter to you, you'll see a side of your child you never thought you'd see. This means that if your teen is interested in music, learn more about music. If your son or daughter is interested in sports, become an expert in that sport. Few things will win someone's trust and admiration faster than being genuinely interested in what he or she is interested in.

This principle applies just as much to the workplace. As a salesperson, if you can connect with the interest of a prospective client and make that important to you, you've probably gained a customer—and maybe even a friend—for life.

CHAPTER FIVE

THE ART
OF LISTENING

When people talk, listen carefully. Most people never listen.
—ERNEST HEMINGWAY

As we continue down the path to becoming masters in human relations, we discover that one of the primary foundations of communication is a genuine interest in others. Without it, communication breaks down before it can ever be productive. Active listening communicates sincere interest more effectively than anything else you can do. Active listening means taking the time and effort to really hear the intent of the person communicating with you.

POWER POINT:
Communication is not monologue,
but dialogue.

Certainly, the very definition of communication implies a two-way connection. Sadly, all too often we think of communication as one person talking while the other person is waiting for his or her turn to talk. The truth is, many times in everyday communication we don't actually hear what the other person is saying. Realizing that the average person can think four times faster than he or she can listen, it's important that we learn to develop a keen listening ear.

You've probably noticed that people often develop their own "dialogues" in their heads while a conversation they should be engaged in is going on. Here's a great example of how we sometimes fail to genuinely listen to others.

The story is told of President Franklin Roosevelt, who often endured long receiving lines at the White House. He complained that no one really paid any attention to what he was saying. One day during a reception he decided to try an experiment. He murmured to each person who passed down the receiving line, "I murdered my grandmother this morning." The guests responded with phrases like, "Marvelous! Keep up the good work." "We are proud of you." "God bless you, Sir." It was not until the end of the line, while greeting the ambassador of Bolivia, that his words were actually heard. Nonplussed, the ambassador leaned over and whispered, "I'm sure she had it coming."[1]

Someone once said, "Good listening is like tuning in to a radio station. For good results, you can listen to only one station at a time. Trying to listen to my wife while looking over an office report is like trying to receive two radio signals at the same time. I end up with distortion and frustration. Listening requires choosing where I will place my attention. To tune in to my partner, I must first choose to put away all that will divide my attention. That might mean laying down the newspaper, moving away from the dishes in the sink, putting down the book I'm reading, or setting aside a project.

By paying rapt attention to another person as she talks I am telling her, "I consider what you have to say as important." It takes time and practice to develop good listening skills. But if you make it a habit, you'll begin to reap the benefits almost immediately. Dale Carnegie, in his book *How to Win Friends and Influence People*, tells the story of a fourteen-year-old store clerk who made it a habit to read the biographies of famous living persons. He would then write personal letters to such individuals as Ralph Waldo Emerson, Louisa May Alcott, and Mary Todd Lincoln, asking them for additional details about their lives. Amazingly, many of the famous individuals he wrote to actually wrote back. Several of them invited him to their homes to talk further. Ultimately the boy established an overnight network of the most influential people in America, simply because he had learned and practiced the art of listening.

> ## POWER POINT:
> Listening is not passive—it's active.

As you develop your listening skills, remember that good listening is not just passively keeping quiet. It is active. This means that you are constantly reading the intent of your partner, and verbally, as well as nonverbally, communicating back that you are engaged in the conversation. It has been said that God gave us each one mouth and two ears for a reason. No one enjoys a motormouth or someone that dominates the conversation. Always be considerate of the other person, and value what he or she is saying even more than your own opinions. Do this, and you'll find yourself with new friends.

The truth is that people care much more about what is happening in their own lives than in the lives of others. So the secret to being a great conversationalist is to ask people questions about themselves, then to be quiet and let them talk about themselves. Because you are willing to listen to them, they will be forever attracted to you.

Listening is not only a good skill for business; it's essential to maintain a healthy marriage and home. Consider the following example. Teenage prostitutes, during interviews in a San Francisco study, were asked: "Is there anything you needed most at home and couldn't get?" Their response, invariably preceded by sadness and tears, was unanimous: "What I needed the most was someone to listen to me, someone who cared enough to listen to me." When was the last time you really took time to listen to your spouse, child, or friend? The next time you find yourself in the middle of a great conversation, try to listen actively, and see if it doesn't change the way you connect with others.

Many problems can be solved, and even prevented, if we

would simply take time to practice active listening. Here are four steps to master this skill:

1. Pause,

2. look,

3. listen, and

4. respond

Pause: When a friend, family member, or coworker approaches you with something to share, stop what you are doing and pay attention. Paying attention, even briefly, lets the other person know that you are listening, and that he or she is important to you.

Look: Be sure to make eye contact with the other person by limiting distractions and directly facing him or her. A pleasant facial expression will encourage others to share their feelings and concerns. As we've previously discussed, look for nonverbal cues that can help you respond accurately to what he or she is trying to say.

Listen: Focus your attention on what he is saying by listening to his words and tone. Listen carefully to what your conversation partner *actually* says as well as what he may be *trying* to say. Mentally "pick up" key words and ideas that will help you better understand that person.

Respond: After you have paused, looked, and listened, it is time to respond. Depending on what the other person has said, an active response might be to paraphrase what you have just heard or ask a question that will lead that person to his or her own solution.

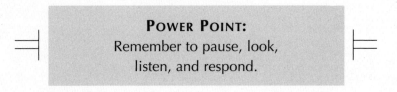

POWER POINT:
Remember to pause, look,
listen, and respond.

It takes a conscious effort to develop a genuine interest in others. Pay close attention the next time you find yourself in the middle of a conversation. Try not to dominate the conversation, and use the listening skills I've outlined in this chapter. Fight the urge to talk about yourself or to interrupt. Focus on the other person. You'll be excited about the results you get.

CHAPTER SIX

THE ART
OF CONVERSATION

The true spirit of conversation consists in building on another man's observation, not overturning it.
— EDWARD BULWER-LYTTON

We've all spent some time in the kitchen reading from a recipe book as we attempt to create something from a list of ingredients. And we've probably all tried to change a recipe with disastrous results. You know the scenario: replace the baking soda with baking powder, or try to prepare chocolate chip cookies without eggs. Well, maybe you haven't—but you can imagine the mess if you did. You've got to have the right ingredients to get the right results. The same is true with a good conversation. To get everything that you can from a conversation, you've got to have all the right ingredients. Here are some of the components that make up a good conversation.

1. Choose your words carefully.

2. Develop a strong vocabulary.

3. Speak the other person's language by asking questions.

4. Discover the power of laughter.

5. Learn to articulate well.

6. Avoid using profanity.

7. Protect the other person's dignity.

1) CHOOSE YOUR WORDS CAREFULLY

Mark Twain put it this way, "The difference between the right word and the almost right word is the difference between lightning and the lightning bug." Words are powerful. Choose them carefully. Organize your thoughts before you speak, and determine which words will best communicate the message you want to send.

POWER POINT:
Choose your words carefully.

One morning, President Franklin Roosevelt asked his secretary to take down a brief message to Congress. As he dictated every word, including punctuation marks, she wrote out, "Yesterday, December 7, 1941, a day that will live in world history, the United States was suddenly and deliberately attacked . . ." After typing the five-hundred-word message, she returned it to

Roosevelt. He made only one change, crossing out "world history" and replacing it with "infamy." As we all know, "a day that will live in infamy" are some of the most famous words ever spoken by a United States president. The right choice of words created a message that will live forever in history.[1]

Roosevelt's British counterpart, Winston Churchill, was also known for his aptly chosen words. The statesman was once on a train, writing a speech about communism. As he looked across the train at a curtain that divided his compartment, he thought up the term "Iron Curtain."

Joseph Conrad once commented, "Words have set whole nations in motion and upheaved the dry, hard ground on which rests our social fabric. Give me the right word and the right accent, and I will move the world."[2]

2) DEVELOP A STRONG VOCABULARY

An intellectual is a man who takes more words than necessary to tell more than he knows.

—JOHN WAYNE

In order to make the right choice of words, you've got to have several different words to choose from. Words represent a powerful arsenal that can be used to accomplish your goals, and it is important that you learn to use them well. One step in this process is to develop a good working vocabulary. Fifty years ago, the average American had a vocabulary of fifty thousand words. Today, that figure is down to a mere fifteen thousand. With the advent of television, the Internet, and other high-tech advances, we have lost the value of a word well spoken.

As John Wayne so aptly noted, no one likes a know-it-all that uses words simply because he knows them. But it is important that you work to expand your vocabulary so that you can easily carry on an interesting conversation within your spheres of influence. There are several books that can be purchased to help you enhance your vocabulary. David Olsen's *The Words You Should Know* will familiarize you with 1,200 words that every educated person should know and use.

While it is important to have a good working vocabulary, it is just as important that you don't overintellectualize conversation. If a person thinks you are "talking down" to him, he will feel that you think you are better than he is. Rather, carefully select the words that will simply communicate your message, and then learn to apply them. A good vocabulary communicates that you value *your* ideas and *the other person's* time.

Consider Lee Iacocca's comments about the leader as a communicator: "It's important to talk to people in their own language. If you do it well, they'll say, 'He said exactly what I was thinking.' And when they begin to respect you, they'll follow you to the death."[3]

3) SPEAK THE OTHER PERSON'S LANGUAGE BY ASKING QUESTIONS

Asking questions is one of the best ways to communicate in the language of the other person. Any good salesperson will tell you the necessity of listening for the interests and needs of a potential client. Salespersons will also tell you how important it is to ask questions based on the information gathered. Asking questions about the other person not only gives you information to improve your selling opportunities, but it helps to communicate a genuine interest in that person.

POWER POINT:
Ask a lot of questions.

Remember to ask questions about his or her personal life as well as his or her professional life. This shows that your concern goes beyond just business, that you care about him or her as a person. You may find a bridge to that person that you never knew existed. You might discover that you went to the same college, that you both enjoy fly-fishing, or that you both have young children at the same school. Strong relationships are based on asking a lot of questions and taking the time to really listen.

Everyone loves to talk about himself or herself. Given the chance, most people can hardly pass up the opportunity to tell you about their experiences, dreams, or triumphs.

4) DISCOVER THE POWER OF LAUGHTER

If you wish to glimpse inside a human soul and get to know a man, don't bother analyzing his ways of being silent, of talking, of weeping, or seeing how much he is moved by noble ideas; you'll get better results if you just watch him laugh. If he laughs well, he's a good man.

—FYODOR DOSTOYEVSKY

Learning to use humor in conversation will greatly enhance your ability to communicate well. Humor and laughter are critical elements to every good conversationalist. Many of the greatest conversationalists of our time were also skilled in using wit and humor to put a person or crowd at ease. Take the following story from the life of Winston Churchill.

As a young statesman, Churchill sported a mustache. One night at a rather formal dinner, he fell into an argument with a woman who, thinking to quell him, snapped, "Young man, I care not for your politics nor your mustache."

"Madam," responded Churchill, "you are unlikely to come into contact with either." This comment eased the tension and allowed the great statesman to continue his conversation.

People love people who laugh. There's something comfortable about someone with an easy laugh, someone who lights up a room with an aptly spoken joke.

Kristi, our youngest daughter, was always the giggly one in our family. I remember one night when Linda was in her last month of pregnancy with David. We had some music playing after dinner, and nine-year-old Kristi grabbed me and started dancing with me. I put my head on her shoulder and she started to laugh. Actually, it was more like a cackle. Hearing Kristi, we all started to laugh and laugh and laugh until our stomachs ached. I thought Linda was going to deliver right there on the spot!

It's always a good idea to keep a few tasteful jokes for appropriate situations. Some people keep a journal of funny stories, writing them down as they hear them. You might not be humorous. But you can change, and you can borrow other peoples' jokes.

Stay away from negative humor and sarcasm. Laughter at someone else's expense inevitably backfires, and leaves a bad taste in people's mouths. They will think to themselves: *If he'll ridicule that person, he'll at some point belittle me.*

Humor and laughter disarm others and endear you to them. A person who is too intense in his communication style makes people uneasy.

POWER POINT:
Laughing at yourself puts
other people at ease.

Preschoolers laugh up to 450 times per day while adults laugh an average of 15 times per day. It's no wonder that preschoolers live healthier, more stress-free lives. Consider this description of laughter:

> The neural circuits in your brain begin to reverberate. Chemical and electrical impulses start flowing rapidly through your body. The pituitary gland is stimulated; endorphins, which are the same chemical make-up as morphine, race through your blood. Your body temperature rises half a degree, your pulse rate and blood pressure increase, your arteries and thoracic muscles contract, your vocal cords quiver, and your face contorts. Pressure builds in your lungs. Your lower jaw suddenly drops uncontrollably, and breath bursts from your mouth at nearly 70 miles an hour.[4]

This is the clinical description of laughter.

POWER POINT:
Learn to laugh easily.

At Northwestern University, a study conducted under strict scientific conditions demonstrated that the act of laughing massages the heart, stimulates blood circulation, and helps the lungs breathe easier. Another test at Fordham University reinforced the conclusion that laughter benefits the heart, lungs, stomach, and other organs. It relaxes our tensions and promotes a feeling of well-being.

Need we say more?

5) LEARN TO ARTICULATE WELL

A conversation is only as good as it is heard. Articulation includes speaking slowly and clearly, as well as completing your thoughts carefully. The bottom line here is this: *Learn to say it clearly.*

A person who talks too fast commonly makes his or her partner feel uncomfortable or rushed. Concentrate on slowing down and delivering a well-spoken message. Speaking slowly will make the person you are trying to communicate with feel more at ease. Fast talkers many times come across as in a hurry or too busy to really care about the conversation at hand.

Some people have developed the annoying habit of not finishing thoughts or sentences. This can be very distracting. It communicates that you aren't really interested in the conversation or the other person. Take the time to concentrate on the words you are saying, and learn to say them slowly and with confidence.

6) AVOID USING PROFANITY

Profanity is the common crutch of the conversational cripple.
—DAVID KEUCK

Profanity indicates a lack of appropriate vocabulary. It can also be a turnoff to people. Remember, your goal is to communicate well to as broad a spectrum of people as possible, and there's no way to know whether or not using profanity will offend the other person. As a rule, it's always better to be safe, and err on the side of the conservative conversationalist.

7) PROTECT THE OTHER PERSON'S DIGNITY

Implement a personal policy to never unnecessarily correct someone else with others around. If someone is telling a story that you know to be inaccurate or providing facts that you would likely challenge, fight the temptation to point out his or her faults in front of other people. If the conversation doesn't rise and fall on the information, let it go. It will do much more for the relationship to look past the misinformation than to publicly challenge or correct that person.

POWER POINT:
Never correct others publicly.

So what do you do when someone really irritates you in public, when an employee rubs you the wrong way in front of your friends, or when a spouse says something that embarrasses you? What do you do? *Nothing!* Chill out. Let it go. Never challenge an employee or spouse in front of other people. Instead, wait for an appropriate time to tell that person in private how you felt. You will win people for life if they know you are willing to protect their dignity in front of their friends.

CHAPTER SEVEN

THE ART
OF AUTHENTICITY

Honesty means integrity in everything. Honesty means wholeness, completeness; it means truth in everything— deed and word.

—ORISON SWETT MARDEN

In communication, it is important to say what you mean and mean what you say—in a way that promotes positive relationships. This is what we call the art of authenticity. The art of authenticity is the mastery of being real with the people around you. A lack of authenticity can lead to strained relationships, where communication is clouded and feelings and intentions are hard to determine. Keeping the lines of communication clear and honest are important elements in relating to others. Here are a few examples of what happens when communication becomes confusing.

Braniff Airlines beckoned its passengers to "Fly in leather." The Spanish translation of that slogan is "Fly naked." Eastern Airlines proclaimed that "We earn our wings daily." In Spanish, that slogan means that their airplanes' final destination would be heaven. General Motors discovered too late that its compact car called the "Nova" literally means "doesn't go" in Spanish. Coors encouraged its English-speaking customers to "Turn it loose"; but this phrase in Spanish means "Suffer from diarrhea." Budweiser's "King of Beers" becomes "Queen of

Beers" in Spanish, because the Spanish word for beer, "cerveza," has a feminine ending.[1]

In the examples above, the intended message was confused because of poor communication and lack of authenticity. The same thing happens when we are unclear about our intentions or play games to manipulate a person.

BE ASSERTIVE

- Do you find it awkward to talk to people you don't know?

- Do you allow other people to cut in front of you at the grocery store?

- Do you eat the food brought to you in restaurants even if it's not prepared properly?

- Do you have trouble communicating what you're really trying to say?

If you answer "yes" to some of these questions, it could be that you need a dose of positive assertiveness. Remember that the words we use communicate important things about us to others. Do your words and actions say that you are confident, or afraid? Do they speak of a positive self-image, or a weak internal voice? Do they tell others that you believe in your product, or that you really don't have an opinion? Do they say,

"Walk on me," or "I'm going somewhere"? Do your words and actions accurately depict the way you feel inside? If not, you're not being real with those around you. Authenticity calls for a certain degree of assertiveness.

> **POWER POINT:**
> Your actions and words fall into one of three categories: passiveness, aggressiveness, or assertiveness.

Passiveness is generally equated with a low self-esteem. This trait allows others to "walk all over us." It exudes weakness and timidity. It lacks the confidence of genuine leadership. Passiveness reflects an inability to communicate what you *actually* think or feel. Examples of passive statements might be

- "I don't care what we do tonight" (when you really do).
- "Whatever you think . . ." (when you have an opinion).

Aggressiveness is one-sided. It fails to take into account the other person's feelings. Aggressiveness usually ends up taking the form of put-downs and sarcasm. It leads to defensiveness and resistance. People don't like to be controlled. Examples of aggressive statements might be

- "No one around here does anything to help."
- "You kids don't appreciate what we do for you."
- "Do it because I say so."

Assertiveness, on the other hand, communicates forthrightness and actually wins people over by empowering them. It is a respect-based balance between passiveness and aggressiveness. It allows you to authentically express your thoughts, feelings, and beliefs without damaging important relationships. It takes into account the other person's viewpoint, and generally leads to cooperation rather than defensiveness. Here are a few keys for developing good assertive skills:

1. Use specifics rather than generalities.
2. Point to behaviors rather than to motives.
3. Remain objective rather than judgmental.
4. Get right to the point.
5. Talk to the right person.

1) USE SPECIFICS RATHER THAN GENERALITIES

- "I just didn't feel good about the presentation."
- "Something about the way you communicate really bothers me."
- "I can't explain what I mean. I just don't like it."

Have you ever had someone communicate in these kinds of generalities, and you had no idea what he or she was talking about? People understand more clearly if we give them specifics. Generalities often make the other person defensive and closed. Specifics provide a fair playing field for others to receive what we're trying to say. As you approach a person about a particular issue, be sure to talk to them clearly about things that are important to the solution of the problem. Talk in terms of individuals (not "someone said"), concrete events, and dates.

> **POWER POINT:**
> Some people say more and more about less and less, and end up saying nothing at all.

2) POINT TO BEHAVIORS RATHER THAN TO MOTIVES

It is very difficult to determine the motives of someone else's heart. When you question motives, you are personally attacking a person. Instead, talk about specific behavior and how that behavior affects how you feel about the issue. Behaviors are measurable, while motives are subjective and can be easily misinterpreted.

3) REMAIN OBJECTIVE RATHER THAN JUDGMENTAL

There is the old story of the Persian king who wanted to teach his four sons never to make rash judgments. So he told the eldest to travel in the winter to see a mango tree, the next to go in the spring, the third in the summer, and the youngest in the fall. After the last son had returned from his autumn visit, the king called them together to describe what they had observed. "It looks like a burnt old stump," said the eldest. "No," said the second, "it is lacy green." The third described it as "beautiful as a rose." The youngest said, "No, its fruit is like a pear." "Each is right," said the king, "for each of you saw the tree in a different season."

The lesson from this story is obvious. Take time to understand, rather than jump to a hasty conclusion. Get the facts straight and try to understand how the other person sees what you're seeing. Remain objective, rather than become judgmental and critical. Keep an open mind as you enter into conversations, and you'll win the attention and affection of those you are talking to. Too often we press our opinions rather than take the time to really listen to the other person. We end up "shutting that person out" and missing potential opportunities.

Nobody likes a critic. People are attracted to people who like and appreciate them, not to people who judge and condemn them. The latter only closes the door of communication.

4) GET RIGHT TO THE POINT

Winston Churchill said, "If you have an important point to make, don't try to be subtle or clever. Use a pile driver. Hit the point once. Then come back and hit it again. Then a third time—a tremendous whack." When it comes to assertiveness, the Prime Minister was right. Don't skirt around issues and confuse your listener. Deal with the real core of the subject. Your listener will appreciate your authenticity and directness. If you're making a sales call, tactfully get to the point. Few things are more annoying than a salesperson who skirts around his pitch. A successful salesperson will be able to sell a potential customer with a concise, to-the-point presentation of the product or service.

5) TALK TO THE RIGHT PERSON

As anyone who has spent time in a garden knows, weeds can be deceptive enemies. In order to get rid of a weed you've got to get to its root, and not just the surface of the plant. The same is true in dealing with people. In order to "get the job done," you've got to get to the right source. This translates into talking to the appropriate person about the issue you're dealing with. Don't waste your time (or the time of the other person) by talking to someone who can't offer you a solution.

As you begin to practice genuine assertiveness, keep in mind that you will probably encounter some aggressive behavior in reaction to you. Be prepared to appropriately handle put-downs and defensiveness with good people skills. But don't give in to the temptation to revert back into a passive posture. You'll rob yourself of the benefits that assertiveness will bring to your situation. Here is an example of appropriate assertiveness: *"When you're late for our appointments, I feel frustrated because it throws off my schedule for the rest of the day. Would it help you if we schedule our Monday meeting at 9:00 rather than 8:00?"*

BE SELF-AWARE

One of the keys to genuine authenticity is seeing yourself accurately, and then determining to continually improve. Other people often see us in a different light than we see ourselves. Learning how to receive correction and make change is an important key to success in life. The more open and authentic you are, the freer people will be in sharing their feelings about you. Don't get defensive. These tips encourage others to help you grow:

1. GIVE YOUR FRIENDS PERMISSION TO TELL YOU THE TRUTH

I once heard someone say that if your enemies are the first to tell you the truth, you don't have any friends. Give your friends permission to be honest with you, and don't punish them when they are. Authentic people are the ones that aren't afraid of knowing when they've made a mistake.

2. DON'T MAKE EXCUSES

For every fault in life, we can find an excuse. Someone put it this way: "An excuse is a lie stuffed with reason." I've often heard the adage, "Losers make excuses; winners make money." Make a conscious effort not to make excuses when someone offers you constructive correction. The greatest leaders in history knew how to receive criticism and then make the necessary changes. Your genuineness is apparent when you take responsibility for a mistake rather than justify it.

3. DON'T BLAME OTHER PEOPLE

Accept responsibility for your actions. Poor communicators and poor leaders blame others for their own faults, and because of this they never seem to find true success in life. It's the ones who accept responsibility and search for change within themselves that become great leaders.

The National Association of Suggestion Systems, a 900-member trade organization based in Chicago, says a quarter of the 1.3 million suggestions received last year by its member companies were used. The result? Companies were able to save more than $1.25 billion, and awarded employees $128 million for their bright ideas.[2]

> ## POWER POINT:
> Constructive criticism has its place.

Abraham Lincoln said, "He has the right to criticize who has the heart to help." It's one thing to simply find fault. But it's an entirely different thing to accurately see problems and offer solutions. When someone gives you constructive input, as long as his or her desire is to genuinely help you, be grateful.

A LAST WORD ABOUT CRITICISM

As you communicate with those around you, understand that if you are doing something significant with your life, you will be criticized. Sometimes you'll be attacked by people who simply want to find fault in everything. The story is told of two taxidermists who stood before a window in which an owl was on display. They immediately began to criticize the way it was mounted—its eyes weren't natural, its wings were not in proportion with its head, its feathers were not neatly arranged, and its feet weren't realistic. When they had finished their critique, the old owl turned his head and winked at them.

It's important to know when to ignore criticism and focus on your goal. The great United States president Theodore Roosevelt made these remarks during a 1910 speech in Paris:

It is not the critic who counts; not the man who points out how the strong man stumbles or where the doer of deeds could have done them better. The credit belongs to the man who is actually in the arena, whose face is marred by dust and sweat and blood; who strives valiantly; who errs, and comes short again and again, because there is no effort without error and shortcoming; but who does actually try to do the deeds; who knows the great enthusiasms, the great devotions, who spends himself in a worthy cause; who at the best knows in the end the triumph of high achievement, and who at the worst, if he fails, at least fails while daring greatly, so that his place shall never be with those cold and timid souls who know neither victory nor defeat.[3]

Never allow another person's opinions to distract you from the thing that you know you are supposed to do. Never allow another's criticisms to deter you from your nobly determined course. Consider the critics, but never live your life by them.

> **POWER POINT:**
> When you stick your head above the crowd, you can expect a few tomatoes thrown your way.
> —JEAN PAUL GETTY

As a student in the school of communication, you'll need to develop a keen skill in the art of authenticity. One of the great challenges to genuine communication is *manipulation*. Manipulation is using a situation or person to unscrupulously achieve a personal advantage. It is having hidden agendas. The fact that they are "hidden" means that there is a lack of authenticity. People often play games to get what they want, rather than communicating openly and honestly.

Some of the games that people play are:

1. THE LYING GAME

The lying game is used to sway the other person's opinion toward your own. The lying game can be played two ways: by omission or by commission. Commission is purposeful or intentional lying to achieve your own personal end. Omission is withholding information that has already been assumed otherwise. The lying game is used to manipulate the other person into believing something is or isn't true in order to get the "upper hand." It is impossible for genuine relationships to survive in this case. Here's an example:

"Mary, why don't you play golf with Jane anymore?" asked a friend.

"Would you play golf with someone who kicked the ball with her foot when you weren't watching?" Mary asked.

"I guess not," admitted the friend.

"Would you want to play with someone who lied about her score?" Mary continued.

"No, I sure wouldn't," the friend agreed.

"Neither did Jane," replied Mary.

No one wants to be involved in the lying game.

2. THE ANGER GAME

The anger game uses negative emotion to manipulate a situation. It hopes to elicit the response "Whatever you want you can have, as long as you don't get angry." The anger game makes people feel they have to "walk on eggshells." In this approach there can be no authenticity in dealing with the issue.

3. THE CRYING GAME

Nothing can end open communication quite like tears. How often have you seen a parent give in to a child once the tears begin to flow? How often have lovers made amends as soon as tears appeared? Certainly, tears are signposts of times of great pain. Unfortunately, tears are sometimes used to manipulate a situation to the benefit of the weeper. Genuine tears are a gift. But manufactured emotion and tears are unhealthy weapons.

4. THE GOD-CARD GAME

Sometimes we hear a person claim that God is telling him to do something. Using the God card is like playing the blame game with God. While divine guidance is certainly important and many times paramount to a good decision, using God to take advantage of a situation is wrong. Putting words in God's mouth is an unfair ploy in authentic communication.

5. THE ROLE GAME

Position and authority are powerful tools in communication. And they should be. When a leader speaks, people listen. In the United States military, when a person of superior rank gives an order, it is followed to the letter without question. In a school system, when a teacher gives a homework assignment, the student usually completes it. We should always strive to honor and obey the authorities in our lives. However, we should never use our own positions or authority to manipulate a situation to our advantage. The greater the position of power, the greater the responsibility to protect the ones we serve. Use authority wisely and authentically, and don't manipulate or play games with the power you've been given.

One of the greatest skills you will need to master to become a great communicator is the art of authenticity. I know it's not easy. You have to be real, and to be willing to tell the truth. But in the long run you'll be happier and more productive in your relationships. Being genuine in relationships will help others to believe what you say, especially when you encourage them.

CHAPTER EIGHT

THE ART OF ENCOURAGEMENT

Those who are lifting the world upward and onward are those who encourage more than criticize.
—ELIZABETH HARRISON

Encouragement: Without it, people often find themselves lost in the mire of life. Without it, companies chug along, barely existing above the bottom line. It is the catalyst to success, the engine of motivation, and the fuel that prepares great leaders. Encouragement has dynamic power. It can be an uplifting word, an aptly given praise, or a well-placed compliment. There is something about a positive word that carries with it a surge of energy. Almost every recognized leader could point back to a significant person who, through a word of encouragement, helped to make his or her dreams come true.

Flatter me, and I may not believe you. Criticize me, and I may not like you. Ignore me, and I may not forgive you. Encourage me, and I will not forget you.
—WILLIAM ARTHUR FORD

UCLA basketball coach John Wooden told players who scored to give a smile, wink, or nod to the player who gave them a good pass. "What if he's not looking?" asked a team member. Wooden replied, "I guarantee he'll look." It's true. We all value and look for encouragement. Learn to become the kind of leader that gives it out regularly and with sincerity.

When we take the time to encourage and empower people in what they are doing, we end up making friends for life. Think back through your own life. The people that have empowered you to accomplish your greatest potential are probably the ones that you still hold in the highest esteem. As you continue on your adventure in the art of communication, you can now add to your communications toolbox the incredible power of encouragement. Physician George Adams found that encouragement is so important, not just to the success of people but to their very well-being, that he often referred to it as "oxygen to the soul."

POWER POINT:
Children are hungry for the approval
and praise of their parents.

One survey asked mothers to keep track of the percentage of times they made negative comments as compared with positive comments to their children. They admitted that they criticized them 90 percent of the time. A three-year survey in one city's schools found that the teachers gave negative comments 75 percent of the time. The study indicated that it takes four positive statements from a teacher to offset the effects of one negative statement to a child.[1] These statistics paint a clear picture of the power of negative input.

Praising your children for doing a good job is a great way to ensure that they'll try even harder the next time. Children are hungry for the approval and praise of their parents. Give praise often and from your heart.

Praise is probably the most economic form of employee motivation available, and also one of the best. In recent surveys, employees almost universally say that the greatest motivation they can get is recognition of a job well done. Praise rewards employees for hard work and increases the chance that they will do quality work in the future.

Praise and encouragement in the workplace has been proven to:

- reinforce a positive organizational culture.

- support company objectives and increase morale.

- retain the top performers.

- increase the overall enjoyment of the workplace.

On the same note, a lack of praise at work will often result in negative morale. People don't want to work for leaders who don't appreciate their hard work. Often, the people left in a negative work environment have a low commitment to the organization, and this is reflected in bottom-line productivity.

Here are some guidelines for delivering praise:

1. ENCOURAGE OTHERS WITH PURPOSE

Solidify in yourself the purpose for giving praise to an employee or family member. Keep in mind that the key purpose for praise is to increase that individual's morale and self-image, to help him be everything he can be. The purpose of encouragement is not to entice everyone to like you. Don't use it just to manipulate a situation to your advantage. Praise should always be given for the benefit of the recipient. You'll reap the rewards as a by-product, with greater productivity or a happier home.

2. FOCUS YOUR PRAISE

When you praise an employee, coworker, or family member, refer to specific accomplishments. Rather than saying "You're a great employee," refer to the particular behavior that you found to be so special.

3. GIVE PRAISE IN PUBLIC

If it won't embarrass an employee, compliment her in front of her coworkers. This will help to improve the overall morale of your organization. A brief mention at a meeting, a blurb in the company newsletter, or a special comment at the dinner table are all great opportunities for public praise. Everyone loves to be admired publicly.

Thomas J. Watson Sr., founder of IBM, was famous for his public acts of recognition. He would often walk around the office with his checkbook out, giving away five, ten, or twenty dollars to people he saw doing a good job. He loved to make a public statement about his employees' good work. The money was insignificant. It was the recognition that mattered. Many of the employees who got a check from Mr. Watson had the check framed and on display. It was the praise that was the real reward, not the money.

PRAISE VERSUS CONDEMNATION

Dale Carnegie once said, "Why don't we try to change people the way we try to change dogs?" To change a dog, we can choose to use either a bone or a whip. If we use the whip, we might change the dog for a short time. But if we use a bone, we will earn the trust and loyalty of the dog. It's the same with people. We can use either condemnation (negative motivations) or praise (positive motivations). Praising people will reap farther-reaching rewards.

However, it's not easy for some of us to practice praising others. *New York Life's* Fred Sievert always struggled with giving sincere compliments to his employees until he had a boss who demonstrated the power of praise. After watching his new boss and emulating what he saw, Sievert said, "It's so simple, and the value it brings is unbelievable. I don't know why I ever resisted stopping and saying, 'You know, I really appreciate you. Thank you for what you've done. I know you've put in a lot of extra time, and believe me, I see it.'" Sievert went on to say, "The comments don't have to be earth-shatteringly large."[2] Take time to acknowledge a job well done. Make an effort to notice the small things in the people's lives around you, and determine to encourage them along the way.

EXTRA-MILE PEOPLE

People will work for money, but they will go the extra mile for praise, encouragement, or recognition. I remember the true story of the man who opened his door to get the newspaper and was surprised to see a strange little dog with his paper in its mouth. Delighted with this unexpected "delivery service," the man fed the pup some treats. The following morning the man was even more surprised to see the same dog in front of his door, wagging his tail, surrounded by eight different neighbors' newspapers. All the dog needed was a bit of encouragement, and he was willing to go the extra mile. When you develop an "extra-mile" mentality, you will begin to break away from the rest of the pack and ensure greater opportunity for success.

GIVING COMPLIMENTS

I can live for a year on a good compliment.

—MARK TWAIN

We all crave words of affirmation. It involves that innate need we talked about earlier, to be appreciated. And a compliment works both ways. A person who gives a compliment feels good that he or she has encouraged another person. And the person who receives the compliment is attracted to the person who's given it. So a rapport and bond develops, which leads to more positive communication.

Everyone likes to be complimented. It builds our confidence and endears others to us. If I'm complimented on my tie, for example, I won't take it off for the next month. If Linda tells me it's sexy, I might even wear it to bed!

You have it easily in your power to increase the sum total of this world's happiness now. How? By giving a few words of sincere appreciation to someone who is lonely or discouraged. Perhaps you will forget tomorrow the kind words you say today, but the recipient may cherish them over a lifetime.

—DALE CARNEGIE

A man attending a seminar on interpersonal relationships became convinced of his need to show appreciation to others.

His wife seemed like an appropriate place to start. So on his way home he picked up a dozen long-stem roses and a box of chocolates. This was going to be a real surprise, and he was excited to begin showing his wife how much he appreciated her.

Arriving home he walked up to the front door, rang the doorbell, and waited for his wife to answer. Immediately upon seeing him, she began to cry. "What's the matter, honey?" asked the confused husband. "Oh, it's been a terrible day," she responded. "First, Tommy tried to flush his diaper down the toilet. Then the dishwasher quit working. Sally came home from school with her legs all scratched, and now you come home drunk!"

Before you develop a reputation for not giving compliments, determine to develop a habit of giving genuine compliments to others. Ken Blanchard, in his bestselling book *The One-Minute Manager*, discusses the value of "one-minute praisings." Thank someone for doing a great job or for being a terrific person. It will go a long way in developing lasting relationships.

POWER POINT:
Give genuine compliments.

Steven Covey, in his book *The 7 Habits of Highly Effective People*, talks about developing an emotional bank account in relationships. The idea is to make an effort to keep a positive balance in the accounts of the people that you communicate with on a regular basis. A genuine compliment, a kind word, a one-minute giving of praise are all positive "deposits" in the emotional bank account. Criticism, put-downs, and accusations are all negative "withdrawals" from that account. Be authentic, but not negative. Positive input is different from criticism.

One survey has found that the biggest complaint among employees is that they only hear about the things that are wrong. They never get words of affirmation and praise about the things they do right.

In marriage, spouses should be each other's greatest cheerleaders and encouragers. A wife will be the most significant determinant factor as to whether her husband will have a good self-image, and vice versa.

When I come offstage after a speech, the first person I look for is Linda. She's always been smart enough to tell me how great I have done, when many times I know that I haven't. She tells me all the time what a great husband I am, and I praise her all the time for being such a wonderful wife. We are each other's most vocal admirers and uplifters. And that's the way it should be.

THE POWER OF HOPE

Any manager or leader can tell you the value of instilling hope, expectancy, and a positive outlook on a group. One of the sacred responsibilities of a good communicator is to instill hope in the people around him or her. Positive communication (speech, thoughts, and actions) is a foundational element in the art of communication. As you influence and communicate with those around you, use positive speech to encourage rather than discourage. Build trust rather than suspicion. Build confidence rather than despair. You have within you a God-given spark of optimism that you are responsible to spread to an often-hopeless society. Author and motivational speaker John Maxwell says, "People will continue working, struggling, and trying if they have hope. Hope lifts morale. It improves self-esteem. It reenergizes people. It raises their expectations."

Great leaders have always understood the power of optimism in the face of despair. Winston Churchill broadcast regularly over the radios of London wonderful messages of hope and optimism during the darkest moments of the Nazi bombing. The people of England were empowered by his encouraging words, and through these inspiring words they were able to overcome unbelievable odds. I challenge you to use the art of encouragement to uplift people to their greatest potential.

CHAPTER NINE

THE ART
OF PROBLEM SOLVING

Don't dwell on what went wrong. Instead, focus on what to do next. Spend your energies on moving forward toward finding the answer.

—DENIS WAITLEY

The American Arbitration Association has recently experienced a massive increase in business. Rental agreements are getting longer. Prenuptial agreements are commonplace. The divorce rate in America is constantly on the increase. In fact, divorced couples in Albuquerque, New Mexico have a new business service to assist their ever-growing numbers. The company is called Freedom Rings: Jewelry for the Divorced. After paying a fee, each customer participates in a ring-smashing ceremony complete with champagne and music. The fact that women are increasingly pounding their wedding rings into pendants, and men are grinding their wedding rings into golf-ball markers is a sad commentary on peoples' inability to communicate effectively and work through problems.

> **POWER POINT:**
> Lack of communication skills is the
> primary reason for marital discord.

Marriage counselors state that the two main reasons for divorce are money problems and communication problems. That statement is only half-true. If peoples' communication skills and problem-solving skills are well-developed, they will be able to work through money problems or any other issues of potential conflict. It really all boils down to the art of problem solving.

No two people will agree on everything. There will always be differences of opinion—that's the nature of human beings. A person will view issues through his or her unique personality and individual past experiences. The key to successful problem-solving communication is to *deal* with an issue of potential disagreement before it turns into a conflict. We can call this employing "preventive medicine" for conflict.

Unfortunately, many of us have used destructive means to deal with potential disagreement, mimicking other people we've seen. With this in mind, let's first list problem-solving methods that *don't* work, so that you can avoid them:

- avoidance

- the silent treatment

- torturous nagging

- ultimatums

- the blame game

- power plays

AVOIDANCE

There are times when the practice of avoidance is beneficial to healthy, harmonious relationships. When someone you're talking with, either alone or in a group, misstates a fact, avoid correcting him unless it's necessary. Think to yourself, "Will his misstatement make a difference five years from now?" If you always argue every point of a discussion, that *could* make a difference five years from now. You will have cultivated distant relationships filled with tension. Major on the majors. Avoid expressing disapproval and disagreement over things that don't really matter.

On the flip side, unfortunately, many people avoid dealing with issues that *do* matter. They are nervous about upsetting the other person and having that person feel badly toward them. This is a destructive use of avoidance. The issue doesn't disappear simply because you don't deal with it. At some point it will rear its ugly head, usually in an explosive and damaging way. Learn to deal with issues of importance. Later in this chapter we will equip you with tools to accomplish this skill.

THE SILENT TREATMENT

As I have already mentioned, some people avoid talking about an issue that is potentially volatile. Other people refuse not only to talk about a certain issue, they simply cut off all communication with the person involved. This not only hurts the relationship, it ends it. The silent treatment can also be used by one person to punish another for disagreeing with him or her. In essence, this "emotional blackmail" is very childish and very destructive. Silence never accomplishes anything except to ensure that the issue in question has no possibility of being resolved.

TORTUROUS NAGGING

This is best exemplified by children with their mothers. "Why can't I go to Susie's? But I want to go to Susie's! Please let me go to Susie's! I should be able to go to Susie's!" And so on, and so on, and so on. The child and mother are in conflict, and the child's strategy is to wear the mother down. Adults have learned to play this same destructive game. It is manipulative, and damages loving relationships. If a person succumbs to such nagging and gives in, he or she does so with resentment. If the person doesn't give in, the nagger is perturbed. It's a no-win situation and an unhealthy way to deal with conflict.

ULTIMATUMS

"I'll give you until Thursday to do what I want. If you don't, you'll be sorry!" Ultimatums are inflammatory and typically cause a "fight-or-flight" response. Nobody likes to be threatened. Communication comes to a screeching halt when a person uses this tactic.

THE BLAME GAME

There is a saying, "The best defense is a good offense." Often when a person feels threatened or attacked, he or she will lash out with a pointing finger: "It's your fault we're in this mess." "It's their fault." "It's my mother's fault." In other words, it's everybody's fault but that person's. This is called *displaced responsibility*, and society has trained us well in this area. We're taught to present ourselves as victims, as if this will somehow give us an edge in a disagreement. Of course, the blame game is a dishonest and ineffective method of problem solving.

POWER PLAYS

One of my business partners phoned me and told me that he had just had an argument with his wife. He explained that he was so upset that he took the engine battery out of her car so that she couldn't drive anywhere. This true story is a perfect example of a power play. Power plays make the statement: "If you don't give me what I want, I won't give you what you want." In marriage, men will often use money as their weapon of power, and women will often use sex. Power plays resolve nothing, and merely exacerbate the problems.

THE ART OF CONFRONTATION

The most successful way to deal with issues of potential disagreement, then, is to *deal* with the issues. This is what we call the "art of confrontation." The reason we label it an "art" is because it involves skill. You are employing non-abrasive techniques as you forthrightly talk about subjects you might not agree on. To become accomplished at talking through issues, it's good for both of you to agree on some foundational principles that will grease the wheels of your discussion.

POWER POINT:
Confront issues in a skillful,
non-abrasive way.

FOUNDATIONAL PRINCIPLE #1

Nothing is a big deal. It is important to maintain an attitude that says, "Nothing is a big deal." There are only "subjects" of discussion, never "problems" of discussion. Anything and everything can be worked out. We are minimizers. We make molehills out of mountains. Nothing is a big deal!

FOUNDATIONAL PRINCIPLE #2

Forgive and forget. As differences of opinion emerge in a discussion, it's nonproductive and unfair for the participants to point out mistakes from the past. Don't be a historian, but rather deal with the issues at hand.

FOUNDATIONAL PRINCIPLE #3

Keep a low tone of voice and speak slowly. It's important that you stay proactive, not reactive, in your emotional tone of voice. If your counterpart is becoming agitated about an issue, strive to maintain your composure. If the other person raises his or her voice, don't react and get sucked into a hyperemotional state. Stay proactive and talk quietly. This will draw his or her speech level down to yours. If the person you're talking to can't collect him- or herself enough to talk rationally, say that you would like to discuss the matter at another time when you can calmly talk about the issue.

FOUNDATIONAL PRINCIPLE #4

Depersonalize everything. "What'd you mean by that?" "That hurt my feelings!" Such comments are frequently heard in the heat of a discussion. Just because a person doesn't like your opinions doesn't mean he or she doesn't like you. And even if a person doesn't like you, as long as you're confident in the position you're taking, this is not your problem.

I learned this long ago from my parents. When I would come home from elementary school complaining about how the school bully was treating me, they would explain that his anger wasn't toward me. "He is probably a very unhappy person. Maybe his parents mistreated him. Instead of being upset with him, we should pray for him, that he has a happier life."

Depersonalize everything.

FOUNDATIONAL PRINCIPLE #5

There are two sides to every story. As you disagree with someone, always be aware that even though you have a strong opinion, your opinion is based on incomplete information. There are always two sides to every story, and you probably don't have all the facts. Certainly, you don't have all the perspectives, since there are always different ways one can assess the facts.

FOUNDATIONAL PRINCIPLE #6

Ask for forgiveness. Even if you believe you were right and the other person was wrong in a disagreement, you can certainly say with sincerity, "I'm sorry if I upset you. That was never my intention. Our relationship is very important to me. I hope you'll forgive me." This will salve the ego of the other person and let her know she is important to you. You may not agree with her, but you do value her.

FOUNDATIONAL PRINCIPLE #7

Never discuss issues of potential conflict on the phone. As we discussed in earlier chapters, your nonverbal communication can be as important, maybe more important, than the words you are speaking. Most of us have gotten off the phone after an uncomfortable discussion thinking *This didn't go the way I had planned*. Unfortunately, now you're off the phone, helpless to mend the bad feelings and miscommunications that have taken place. If there's a controversial topic you're confronting, it's important to deal with the other person face-to-face.

FOUNDATIONAL PRINCIPLE #8

Never talk about anything important when you're tired. Many of us as married couples find that our worst arguments come late at night. When you're tired, you view things differently, in a more distorted fashion. When you're rested, birds are chirping, the sun is shining, and everything appears in a more positive light. Agree that if either party is tired, you'll put off your discussion until a better time.

WHAT IF A CONFLICT ISN'T GETTING RESOLVED?

If two persons can't work through their differences, it's not because the problem is insurmountable; it's because they haven't developed their problem-solving and communication skills. If this is the case, bring in a third party to help mediate the discussion.

> **POWER POINT:**
> When communication is at an impasse,
> seek a third-party counsel.

YOU CAN'T TAKE IT WITH YOU

There is the familiar saying, "You can't take it with you." This means you can't take your house or your boat or your money with you to heaven. Scripture tells us, though, that there is one thing that you can take with you: *relationships!* Relationships can be a source of your greatest joy or your deepest heartbreak. The art of problem-solving will allow you to develop harmonious, loving relationships that will be your greatest joy.

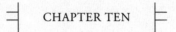

CHAPTER TEN

THE ART OF NLP

Insanity is continuing to do the same thing expecting different results.

—ALBERT EINSTEIN

Neurolinguistic Programming (NLP) is a relatively new science. It includes a number of techniques that will help you to communicate more effectively.

The prefix *neuro* means "mental." *Linguistic* refers to language, both spoken and unspoken. *Programming* is a computer term for a recurring method for dealing with a problem. A big part of NLP is understanding the power, meaning, and associations that our words can produce. Three power principles of NLP are

1. the power of goals

2. building rapport

3. understanding representational systems[1]

THE POWER OF GOALS

One of the key tenets of NLP is that the more specifically we define what we want, the more likely our "programmed" minds will create an environment to satisfy those desires.

When Lia, our oldest daughter, was twelve, she entered a citywide track meet. A week before her big race, she explained how nervous she was getting about losing. I suggested that she close her eyes a couple of times a day and visualize herself breaking the ribbon as she crossed the finish line first. A few days before the track meet she excitedly explained at breakfast that the night before she had had a dream of crossing the finish line in first place. Several days later, we proudly watched as Lia broke the ribbon.

> **POWER POINT:**
> If you don't know where you're going,
> you're not going to like where you end up.

As you enter into conversations with people, it's important that you determine the objectives of your interaction. Is your goal to create a connection where they feel good about you? Is it to complete a sale? Is it to win them over to your way of thinking? If you are specific in your understanding of what you want, your chance of leaving the discussion having realized these goals is increased exponentially.

Of course, the same thing is true in the other areas of your life. Fifteen percent of people have a clear idea of what they want in life. Three percent write these goals down. And people in that three percent are generally the achievers in life.

Keep your goals in front of you every day, whether it's a list on your mirror or a page in the front of your day planner. The more specific you are, the better chance you have to reach the desired outcome. Break up your large goals into small daily tasks.

POWER POINT:
How do you eat an elephant?
One bite at a time.

BUILDING RAPPORT

NLP seeks to help people develop the ability to understand and respond to other people's models of the world. This rapport will come from your understanding their representational systems, which we'll discuss in the next section. But it also comes from your awareness of their body language and tone of voice.

POWER POINT:
Mirror a person, and he will unconsciously feel more connected with you.

Good communication requires that you validate the other person's feelings and ideas. One of the best ways to do this is to mirror him or her. If a person is talking with a quiet and slow cadence, you do the same thing. That person will unconsciously feel a rapport with you, without even understanding why.

It's the same with body language. If a person across from you is sitting in an engaging position with her hands extended across the table, try sitting the same way. If she is sitting with her hands on her lap, do the same with yours. If she has a big grin, you smile. If she raises her eyebrows, you raise yours. Through mirroring, the person you are communicating with will sense that you and she—or he—are in tune with one another.

UNDERSTANDING REPRESENTATIONAL SYSTEMS

People use different representational systems as their *primary* basis for thoughts and feelings. It's helpful in creating a connection with a person that you identify the other person's preferred representational system, and communicate with him from that perspective. There are five representational systems, though the first three are the most commonly used: visual (sight), auditory (hearing), kinesthetic (touch), olfactory (smell), and gustatory (taste). Here are some examples of how to work with these different perspectives:

Sight: "Can you *see* what I mean?"

Hearing: "Do you *hear* what I'm saying?"

Touch: Can you *grasp* what I'm talking about?"

Here are three accounts from three different perspectives of a couple strolling down the beach with their ten-year-old son. Keep in mind that the wife is kinesthetic, the husband is visual, and the son is auditory in their preferred representational systems.

The wife remembers . . .

I'll never forget the day at the beach. I remember the warmth of the sun as it shone on our faces and wrapped itself around us. I remember the fine, cooling sand as it held our feet every time we touched the ground. I remember the strength of my husband's hand as he reached out to hold mine. I remember the embrace of my son as he threw his arms around my waist. I remember feeling safe and warm and special. I'll never forget that day.

The husband remembers . . .

I'll never forget the day at the beach. I remember how the sun glowed on the horizon as it began to slowly set over the glistening water. I remember the hundreds of lines the waves had carved onto the beach as reminders of the timeless tide. I remember the sudden beauty of my wife as she smiled in the fading sunlight. I remember the look in my son's eyes as he ran to show us a prize-winning shell. It was more than my eyes could absorb. I'll never forget that day.

The son remembers . . .

I'll never forget the day at the beach. I remember the sound of the waves as they crashed gently onto the shore. I remember the cry of the seagulls as they circled above us, waiting for a handout. I remember listening to my mom and dad laugh and talk as I sloshed quietly behind them, whistling to myself. I remember the sounds of the ocean, and also the absolute quiet of the beach. I remember saying to myself, "Now, this is paradise." And it was. I'll never forget that day.

In these accounts, all three lived through the same scenario, but all three experienced it differently, through the lens of their preferred representational systems. If you can learn to pinpoint how those around you experience the world, and really try to experience the same world they do, you'll be amazed at how effective your communication will become.

All of the principles taught in NLP aim to make you more

relatable as a communicator. Remember, communication does not take place by your merely talking at someone. Your words must be *received*, and the person you're talking to must be receptive.

> *The greatest problem with communication is the illusion that it has been accomplished.*
> —GEORGE BERNARD SHAW

CHAPTER ELEVEN

THE ART
OF SELF-TALK

Whether you think you will succeed or not, you are right.
　　　　　　　　　　　　　　　　　　　—HENRY FORD

Who is the person you communicate with the most? Your spouse? Your child? A coworker at your job? No, the person you spend the most time talking to is yourself. This is called "self-talk." It is our self-talk, then, that is most influential in determining our self-images, our happiness, and ultimately our legacies once we have completed our journey here on Planet Earth.

> **POWER POINT:**
> The subconscious mind will use all its available resources to actualize what it believes.

Scripture states, "As [a person] thinks in his heart, so *is* he" (Proverbs 23:7 NKJV). If I tell myself that I will never find happiness, or that life is tough and "I'm a victim of my past," my subconscious mind receives what I tell myself and ensures through my actions that I fulfill my negative expectations.

POWER POINT:
The subconscious mind accepts everything
the conscious mind is thinking—good and bad.

If, on the other hand, I think to myself, "My past does not determine who I am. I determine my destiny through my choices and actions. I choose to be happy and win in the game of life," then my subconscious mind goes to work to move me toward a life of fulfillment and victory.

So it would appear, then, that we are at the mercy of our thoughts as they arbitrarily move through our minds, reacting to external stimuli. But no, we have been given the ability to choose what we think and to control our thoughts. Animals only have the ability to be reactive. When a bull looks across the pasture and sees a cow, it starts running after it with its tongue hanging out. That's what animals do—they react.

Human beings, on the other hand, are different. They have the ability to take initiative and be proactive. They can control their thoughts and emotions. As a parallel example, when a man sees a woman across the pasture, he does not run after her with his tongue hanging out. He says to himself, "I'm married. I love my wife. I'm not supposed to run after other women with my tongue hanging out. I can control my thoughts and my emotions, and I need to."

POWER POINT:
Take responsibility for your
thoughts and emotions.

We need to learn to take responsibility for our thoughts, rather than allow them to float through our minds in an uncontrolled fashion. As we stated in an earlier chapter, we live in a society of displaced responsibility. "It's not my fault I shot three people at a fast-food restaurant. It's my mother's fault. She locked me in a closet for eight hours when I was five years old." The last thing we take responsibility for is our thoughts and emotions: "That's just how I feel! I can't forgive him. I'm just too upset!" If you take responsibility for your thoughts and emotions, and accept that you are a human being and not an animal, then you'll begin to change your vocabulary. You'll say, "I *choose* not to forgive him. I *choose* to be upset." Thoughts and emotions are choices you make every minute of every day.

POWER POINT:
Continually observe what you're
thinking and feeling.

So we must constantly be vigilant as we observe our self-talk. Periodically, we must reside outside of ourselves. We must watch our thought patterns. This is the first step to controlling our own thoughts and emotions. We must be aware of them.

> **POWER POINT:**
> You can't have emotions without first
> having thoughts that lead
> to these emotions.

Let's begin with controlling our emotions. Have you ever looked out of the window of an airplane as the airplane bounced around in bad weather? You probably noticed that the steel wings bent up and down in the turbulence, and you most likely thought, "The steel wings are bending up and down? Steel isn't supposed to bend. Those wings could snap off!" Suddenly you were gripped with fear that you were going to die. So your thoughts lead to emotions. How, then, do you control your emotions? You control your emotions by controlling your thoughts.

> **POWER POINT:**
> The mind can't think two thoughts at once.

When you notice unproductive thoughts blossoming in your mind—thoughts that lead you away from what you want in life, such as happiness, success, and so forth—displace those thoughts with positive self-talk. In the example of the airplane whose wings were bending in turbulent weather, you start telling yourself, "Thousands of airplanes fly in bad weather every day without any problems. Their wings bend also, and they don't crash. Airplanes are safer than automobiles. I'm better off here than I am in a car."

Because you have chosen to replace the negative thoughts with positive self-talk, and because the mind can't think two thoughts at once, there is no room for the fearful thoughts that lead to fearful feelings.

I've been through some terrible things in my life, some of which actually happened.

—MARK TWAIN

POWER POINT:
Break your negative patterns of thinking.
It's your choice.

Some people spend their entire lives living with an attitude like that of Snoopy, the cherished Peanuts cartoon pet. Snoopy sat droopy-eyed at the entrance of his doghouse lamenting, "Yesterday I was a dog. Today I'm a dog. Tomorrow I'll probably still be a dog. *Sigh*. There's so little hope for advancement." Many people, like Snoopy, have developed negative patterns of thought. You've probably heard the expression, "He's looking through rose-colored glasses." We need to *choose* to view the world through rose-colored glasses. We should choose to see the glass as half-full, as opposed to half-empty. We ought to choose to see ourselves as happy and successful in all areas of life. These are choices. When you think to yourself, *They don't care what I have to say,* displace those thoughts with, *I have valuable ideas that they will want to hear about!* Because the mind can't think two thoughts at once, you will begin to feel that you are a person of value.

POWER POINT:
Write down positive self-talk affirmations
that you can read out loud.

If you're saying, "I can't think of anything positive to tell myself," try writing down on paper positive statements or affirmations you can read aloud to yourself. You may even want to compose a mission statement, a positive purpose as to what you want to accomplish with your life. When destructive thoughts of doubt and fear creep into your mind, immediately read your mission statement and displace those thoughts.

We have a sign above our kitchen sink: "Be Happy—A Decision." Linda periodically has to remind herself that I don't make her happy or unhappy, our children don't make her happy or unhappy, our finances don't make her happy or unhappy. She determines whether she will be happy or unhappy by the thoughts she chooses to think.

POWER POINT:
Make a choice to rejoice.

It is a good idea to write down a list of all the things that you're grateful for. When you start to feel discouraged, after thinking discouraging thoughts, read your list of blessings. Have an "attitude of gratitude," and displace the discouragement.

Most people are about as happy as they make up their minds to be.

—ABRAHAM LINCOLN

Understanding and applying the principles in this chapter will empower you to experience a rewarding life full of joy and achievement. The art of self-talk, above all else, is the secret to your success here on Planet Earth.

EPILOGUE

The tongue of the wise brings healing.
—PROVERBS 12:18 NRSV

The world-famous author Dale Carnegie discovered the enormous need for effective communication skills when he placed an ad in a New York newspaper promoting a meeting on that subject. On the night of the meeting, he walked into a hotel room overflowing with twenty-five hundred eager people. Even in the midst of the Great Depression, these people understood that something more than the book knowledge acquired at college is needed to succeed in business and life. They packed into that room because they had a hunger to be better communicators. In the same way, you've opened this book because you have a hunger to be a better communicator.

Congratulations! You've successfully completed this course in the art of communication. If you apply the ideas and principles that you've discovered in this book, you will begin to see a dramatic change in the way you interact with others and in the overall success of your life. The old saying is true: "How much you earn is determined by how much you learn." Let's take a minute to review what you've learned.

Don't forget: The secret ingredient in the recipe for success of many outstanding people is that they learned to master the art of communication.

The *art of unspoken language* is a key to skillful communication. Developing a keen sensitivity to the nonverbal signals of others can make all the difference in our relationships.

The next time you step up to the mirror, remember the principles you've learned in the *art of appearance*. Remember that clothing always communicates. Remember that overdressing is always better than underdressing. Clothes and appearance don't make you, but they might keep someone else from making a decision that could affect your life!

You'll become a hero at work if you'll practice the *art of valuing others*. Few things will endear you to others more than genuine empathy. If you determine to see situations from the perspective of others, you'll be amazed at the effectiveness of your communication skills. One of the greatest ways to ensure your own success in life is to help someone else achieve his or hers!

Slow down. Don't merely let someone else talk, but listen actively. Most of the time, the secret to a winning conversation is wrapped somewhere in the words and emotions of the person you are talking to. Develop the *art of listening* to help you identify the real needs and feelings of those around you, and your interactions will be more successful.

The *art of conversation* is a lot like painting. As you gain confidence in conversation, you'll begin to experiment with new techniques, words, and ideas. Just as it takes practice and time to become a gifted artist, it takes practice and time to develop winning conversation skills. Remember to put into practice the principles you've learned in Chapter 6, and make it your goal to become a skilled conversationalist.

Nothing will win the hearts of those around you like the *art of authenticity*. People are anxious to know the *real* you. Take the risk to let others into your world. You have the skills and knowledge to be an excellent communicator. Don't be afraid to confidently and genuinely engage those around you.

Remember to practice the *art of encouragement* with those at home and work. If you have children at home, take time today to encourage them. At work tomorrow, take time to give genuine compliments to those with whom you interact. Begin to use this powerful tool for empowering relationships, and you'll reap the benefits.

We all know that communication is not always easy. In fact, it can be very difficult and often frustrating. Don't get discouraged by challenges in relationships. Take the skills you've learned in the *art of problem solving*, and begin to apply them to your life and circumstances. Begin to practice the small things. Don't blame. Don't nag. Take responsibility. Look for the win/win resolution to a problem. Become a problem solver.

The *art of NLP* is a new and exciting science that will help you develop empowering relationships. Use the skills and techniques you've learned in this chapter to create rapport with people. You will, without question, enhance your relationships and your overall communication skills.

Don't forget to practice the *art of self-talk!* Successful communication really begins with the most important conversation you'll have today, the conversation you have with yourself. Understanding this will allow you to feel better about yourself and hence to enjoy more meaningful relationships with those around you.

But your journey is only just beginning.

It's been said that a journey of a thousand miles begins with a single step. And the hardest step is the first one. When it comes to effective communication, this couldn't be truer. Having all the success secrets in the world doesn't mean a thing unless you are willing to take the first steps to actually practice them. And as you do, your relationships will become more satisfying and your life will be more fulfilled.

NOTES

CHAPTER ONE

1. *Crossroads*, Issue 7, 15–16.
2. Joe White, *Homemade*, November 1989.
3. *Daily Mirror*, (London).

CHAPTER TWO

1. Plutarch, *Lives of the Ten Orators* (A.D. 46?-A.D. c. 120).
2. *Bits and Pieces*, 3 March 1994, 11.
3. Hadden W. Robinson, *Biblical Preaching* (Grand Rapids, Mich: Baker Book House, 2001), 193.
4. William Danforth, *I Dare You* (I Dare You Committee, 1974), 38.

CHAPTER THREE

1. Peggy Post, *Emily Post's Etiquette* (New York: Harper Collins, 1997), 698.
2. Michael Broome, *Bosom Buddy*.

CHAPTER FOUR

1. *Today in the World*, Feb. 1991, 10.

CHAPTER FIVE

1. Clifton Fadiman and Andre Bernard, eds., *Bartlett's Book of Anecdotes* (New York: Little Brown & Company, 2000), 465.

CHAPTER SIX

1. *Bartlett's Book of Anecdotes*, 465.
2. Glenn Van Ekeren, *Speaker's Sourcebook II* (Saddle River, N.J.: Prentice Hall Press, 1993), 73.
3. Ibid.
4. Ibid., 222.

CHAPTER SEVEN

1. *American Demographics*, Feb. 1992, 1.
2. *Management Digest*, Sept. 1989.
3. Theodore Roosevelt, address delivered at the Sorbonne, Paris, 23 April 1910.

CHAPTER EIGHT

1. Institute of Family Relations, *Homemade*, Dec. 1986.
2. Dale Carnegie and Associates, *The Leader in You* (Crofton, Md.: Poseidon Press, 1993), 129.

CHAPTER TEN

1. Joseph O'Connor and John Seymour. *Introducing NLP.* (Wellingborough, UK: Thorsons Publishers, 2000).

ABOUT
THE AUTHOR

Over the past twenty-five years, TERRY FELBER has built a sales organization that numbers more than 50,000 people. He regularly speaks to large audiences around the world about the principles of successful communication, equipping his listeners with techniques to achieve more fulfilling relationships. He and his wife, Linda, reside in Colorado and Florida.